ARNE HEROLD

MENTAL ILLNESSES

From A-Z

Mental illness remains a challenge for millions of people worldwide, despite advances in medical research and treatment technologies.

Epidemiological studies show that psychiatric illnesses have a significant impact on individual well-being, as well as on health systems and society as a whole. In many countries, they are among the leading causes of disability and inability to work.

Likewise, they often remain burdened with prejudices and misunderstandings. People who suffer from a mental disorder often face prejudice and discrimination, whether at work, at school, or in the social environment. This can lead to those affected isolating themselves and not seeking the help they need.

In this book , you will learn about their causes, symptoms, and treatment options for these diseases. We hope that this will help to develop a better understanding of the complexity and diversity and to reduce prejudices so that those affected can receive appropriate support and help. We would like to encourage people to have an open and empathetic dialogue about mental health and to find ways together to better support people with psychiatric illnesses as a society.

TABLE OF CONTENTS

ADDICTION

ICD-10 Code: F10-F19

Addiction is a mental illness characterized by the compulsive craving for a substance or behavior, despite negative consequences or knowledge of potential harm. People with an addiction often have difficulty controlling their use and experience withdrawal symptoms when they try to reduce or quit the addictive substance.

Addictions can take a variety of forms, including:

1. Substance dependence: This includes the excessive use of substances such as alcohol, tobacco, illegal drugs, prescription drugs, or other addictive substances that can lead to physical dependence, tolerance, and withdrawal symptoms.

2. Behavioral addictions: These include compulsive behaviors that are not focused on a substance but on a specific behavior, such as gambling, internet use, gambling addiction, excessive shopping, workaholism, or eating disorders.

The causes of addictions can include a combination of genetic, biological, psychological, social, and environmental factors. These include genetic predispositions, neurochemistry, mental health problems, traumatic experiences, stress, social isolation, availability of addictive substances, peer pressure or unfavorable living conditions.

Treatment for addictions often involves a combination of drug therapy, psychotherapy, and behavioral interventions. Medications can be used to relieve withdrawal symptoms, reduce cravings, or treat underlying mental health conditions. Psychotherapy, such as cognitive behavioral therapy (CBT), motivational interviews, 12-step programs, or support groups, can help identify, process, and manage harmful patterns of behavior and develop healthy coping strategies.

Addictions are often chronic and prone to relapse.

ADDICTION DISORDER

ICD-10 Code: F10-F19

An addiction disorder is a disorder that greatly affects an individual's life by creating a compulsive and often uncontrollable attachment to a particular substance or behavior. This condition is often accompanied by a strong desire or urge to consume the substance or behavior, even if it has negative consequences for physical health, psychological stability, or social relationships.

People who suffer from addiction often show a pattern of continued use despite knowing the harmful effects. The urge to consume the substance or behavior can be so overwhelming that they have difficulty controlling or limiting their use, even if they are aware that they could suffer harm.

This condition can take a variety of forms, including substance dependence (such as alcohol, drugs, or prescription drugs) or behavioral dependence (such as gambling, internet use, or work). Regardless of the specific form, an addiction disorder often manifests itself through withdrawal symptoms when the use of the substance or behavior is interrupted, as well as the development of tolerance, as a result of which the person needs progressively larger amounts of the substance or behavior to achieve the desired effect.

Addiction disorders can have a serious impact on various areas of life, including physical health, mental stability, interpersonal relationships, and professional performance. Treatment often requires a multidisciplinary approach that includes medical intervention, psychotherapy, social support, and possibly participation in support groups.

ADHD

ICD-10 Code: F90.0

ADHD stands for attention deficit hyperactivity disorder, a neurodevelopmental disorder that manifests itself as impairments in attention, impulsivity, and hyperactivity. People with ADHD may have difficulty focusing their attention on a specific task for long periods of time, acting impulsively, and feeling an excessive urge to move.

This disorder often begins in childhood and can persist into adulthood. It can affect various areas of life, including academic performance, interpersonal relationships, and professional functionality.

Typical symptoms of ADHD include restlessness, impulsivity, inattention, difficulty organizing tasks, lack of perseverance in boring or repetitive tasks, and an increased risk of impulsive behavior or accidents.

The exact causes of ADHD are not fully understood, but both genetic and environmental factors are thought to play a role. Treatment for ADHD often involves a combination of medication, behavioral therapy, parent training, and support from schools or work environments. Early diagnosis and intervention can help alleviate symptoms and allow people to achieve their full quality of life.

ADJUSTMENT AND STRESS DISORDERS

ICD-10 Code: F43.2

Adjustment and stress disorders are mental disorders that occur in response to stressful life events. These events can be of a different nature, such as the loss of a loved one, a breakup, professional stress, moving, health problems, or financial difficulties. People with adjustment and stress disorders have difficulty adapting to these changes, which can lead to emotional distress, functional impairment and personal suffering.

The symptoms of adjustment and stress disorders can be diverse and range from emotional reactions such as anxiety, depression, anger, irritability or hopelessness to physical complaints such as headaches, stomach problems or sleep disorders. Symptoms can vary depending on the individual reaction to the stressful event and personal coping mechanisms.

Adjustment and stress disorders are usually temporary and generally subside as the person begins to adapt to the new circumstances and develop coping strategies. However, in some cases, symptoms can persist and lead to long-term distress, especially if the stressful event is particularly traumatic or severe, or if the person does not have sufficient coping skills.

The diagnosis of adjustment and stress disorders is made by a clinical evaluation by a qualified professional, such as a psychiatrist or psychologist. This usually involves a thorough medical history to identify the stressful event, an evaluation of symptoms and their impact on daily life, and a differential diagnosis to rule out other mental disorders.

Treatment for adjustment and stress disorders usually focuses on helping the affected person cope with the stressful event and developing healthy coping strategies. This can be achieved through psychotherapy, especially cognitive behavioral therapy

(CBT) or supportive therapy, to improve coping skills and change negative thought patterns. If necessary, short-term drug treatments such as antidepressants or anxiety relievers may also be prescribed to alleviate acute symptoms and improve functioning.

AGGRESSION

ICD-10 Code: F63.81

Aggression refers to a pattern of behavior characterized by hostility and a desire to harm or dominate. This behavior can be both verbal and physical and can occur in different contexts, including interpersonal conflict, territorial defense, or frustration. People who are aggressive can display a variety of expressions, from overt anger to more subtle forms such as sarcasm or passive-aggressive behavior.

Aggression can be divided into two main categories: instrumental aggression and hostile aggression. Instrumental aggression refers to aggressive behavior that serves as a means to achieve a specific goal, such as defending one's territory or asserting personal interests. Hostile aggression, on the other hand, springs from a deeper sense of hostility or anger and aims to harm or humiliate the other, often without a clear purpose or benefit.

It is important to note that aggression is not necessarily negative. In some situations, it can even perform adaptive functions, such as in self-defense or in the fight for resources. However, excessive or uncontrolled aggression can lead to significant problems, especially in social relationships or in society as a whole.

The causes of aggression are varied and can include biological, psychological and social factors. Biological factors such as genetic predisposition, neurotransmitter imbalances or hormonal influences can play a role, as can psychological factors such as frustration tolerance, impulse control or traumatic experiences in childhood. Social factors such as family dynamics, cultural norms, or socioeconomic circumstances can also contribute to the development of aggression.

Treatment for aggression depends on the underlying cause and severity of the problem. Therapeutic approaches such as cognitive behavioral therapy, anger management, or family therapy can be helpful in identifying and modifying the underlying emotional or interactive patterns. In some cases, medication, especially to treat comorbidities such as depression or anxiety disorders, can also be used to relieve symptoms and improve emotional regulation.

ALCOHOLISM

ICD-10 Code: F10.2

Alcohol dependence, also known as alcoholism or alcohol addiction, is a condition characterized by an uncontrollable and compulsive use of alcohol, despite the negative effects on physical health, social life, and other areas of life. People who are addicted to alcohol develop a tolerance to alcohol, which means they have to drink larger and larger amounts to achieve the same effects. They also experience withdrawal symptoms when they try to reduce or stop their alcohol consumption.

The causes of alcohol dependence are diverse and can include genetic, psychological, social and environmental factors. People with a family history of alcoholism are at a higher risk of becoming addicted to alcohol themselves, which could indicate a genetic predisposition. Psychological factors such as stress, anxiety, depression, or traumatic life events can also contribute to the development of alcohol dependence, as alcohol is often used as a coping mechanism. Social factors such as peer pressure, social acceptance of alcohol consumption or availability of alcohol also play a role.

Symptoms of alcohol dependence can vary, but they often include a strong craving for alcohol, difficulty controlling alcohol consumption, neglect of obligations due to drinking, progressive development of tolerance, withdrawal symptoms such as tremors, nausea or anxiety when alcohol consumption is reduced, as well as continued alcohol consumption despite the negative consequences for health, relationships or professional performance.

Treatment for alcohol dependence usually requires a holistic approach that includes medical, psychological, and social interventions. Detoxification and medical monitoring may be necessary to manage withdrawal symptoms and prevent potentially life-threatening complications. Subsequently, long-term therapy, including behavioral therapy, group therapy, or 12-step programs such as Alcoholics Anonymous, can help manage the psychological and social causes of addiction and support relapse prevention. The use of medications such as naltrexone or acamprosate can also help support abstinence in some cases by reducing the craving for alcohol or mitigating the negative effects of alcohol consumption.

ALZHEIMER'S
ICD-10 Code: G30.9

Alzheimer's disease is a progressive neurodegenerative disease that impairs cognitive function and leads to a gradual loss of memory, thinking ability, and behavior.

It is the most common form of dementia and usually affects the elderly, although it can also occur in younger adults.

Alzheimer's disease is characterized by the formation of abnormal protein deposits in the brain, including beta-amyloid plaques and tau protein tangles. These deposits disrupt normal communication between nerve cells and ultimately lead to the death of neurons, leading to a progressive loss of cognitive function.

The symptoms of Alzheimer's disease develop slowly and insidiously. Early signs include memory loss, especially difficulty remembering newly acquired information, as well as problems with thinking, language, orientation, and judgment. As the disease progresses, symptoms may worsen, with sufferers potentially having difficulty performing everyday tasks, developing problems communicating, and experiencing changes in behavior and personality.

The diagnosis of Alzheimer's is based on a thorough clinical evaluation, including a comprehensive medical history, physical exams, neuropsychological tests, and brain imaging. There is currently no cure for Alzheimer's disease, but treatments can help relieve symptoms and slow the progression of the disease. This may include the use of medications such as cholinesterase inhibitors and memantine, which help improve the function of certain neurotransmitters in the brain and alleviate the symptoms of Alzheimer's disease. In addition, non-drug therapy such as cognitive rehabilitation, occupational therapy, and caregiver support can help improve the quality of life of people with Alzheimer's and maintain their independence in daily life.

Caring for people with Alzheimer's requires a holistic approach that aims to address their physical, emotional, and social needs. Relatives of Alzheimer's patients often need support and training to deal with the challenges of care and take care of their own needs.

AMNESIA

ICD-10 Code: F44.0

Amnesia refers to a condition in which a person loses parts or all of their memory, including remembering personal experiences, facts, or learned knowledge. This loss of memory can be temporary or permanent and can have various causes, including traumatic events, neurological disorders, psychiatric illnesses or medical conditions.

There are several types of amnesia, including retrograde amnesia, anterograde amnesia, and dissociative amnesia. Retrograde amnesia refers to the loss of memory content that occurred before a specific event or injury, while anterograde amnesia refers to the loss of the ability to form new memories after a certain point in time. Dissociative amnesia occurs when a person blocks memories of stressful or traumatic events, often as a protective mechanism against emotional overload.

The symptoms of amnesia can vary depending on the cause and severity. The most common signs include memory loss, disorientation, difficulty learning new information, confusion about one's identity or environment, and problems remembering past events or personal details.

Diagnosing amnesia requires a comprehensive clinical evaluation by a doctor, including a medical history, physical exams, and possibly neuropsychological testing or brain imaging to determine the underlying cause of memory loss.

Treatment for amnesia depends on the underlying cause and may include a combination of medical interventions, psychotherapy, and rehabilitation. Medications may be prescribed to treat conditions such as Alzheimer's disease, stroke, or brain injury that can cause memory loss. Psychotherapeutic approaches such as cognitive behavioral therapy or trauma-based therapy can be helpful in processing stressful events and restoring the ability to remember. In addition, participating in rehabilitation programs that promote cognitive and functional skills, including memory training and life skills, can help improve the independence of people with amnesia.

ANOREXIA/ANOREXIA NERVOSA
ICD-10 Code: F50.0

Anorexia, also known as anorexia nervosa, is a mental illness characterized by an extreme fear of gaining weight, a disturbed body image, and highly restrictive food intake. People with anorexia often have a distorted body image and consider themselves overweight, even if they are underweight. You may compulsively count calories, engage in excessive physical activity, or use unhealthy weight-loss methods, such as fasting, vomiting, or abusing laxatives or diuretics.

Symptoms of anorexia can be physical, emotional, and social, and include:

- Extreme underweight that is disproportionate to height and age
- Intense fear of gaining weight or fear of becoming obese despite an already low weight
- Strict diet and eating habits that lead to highly restrictive food intake
- A distorted body image and an excessive focus on body weight or shape
- Excessive physical activity or exercise to burn calories or avoid weight gain
- denial of the seriousness of one's weight loss or the effects of restrictive food intake, and

- Physical symptoms such as fatigue, dizziness, hair loss, brittle nails, dry skin, muscle weakness or amenorrhea (absence of menstruation).

The causes of anorexia are multifactorial and include genetic predisposition, psychological, social, and cultural factors, as well as a combination of environmental factors such as stress, trauma, perfectionism, low self-esteem, and societal pressure to be thin.

The treatment of anorexia requires a multidisciplinary approach that includes medical, psychotherapeutic and nutritional interventions. The aim of treatment is to normalize weight, improve food intake, change unhealthy attitudes towards food and the body, treat psychological problems.

Coping with anorexia requires long-term treatment and support, as well as the involvement of family and other supporters. Early detection, early intervention and comprehensive, holistic treatment are crucial for recovery and the prevention of serious complications associated with anorexia.

ANXIETY DISORDER

ICD-10 Code: F41.1

An anxiety disorder is a mental illness characterized by excessive and persistent anxiety or worry that goes beyond what would be appropriate in a given situation. People with anxiety disorders often experience intense and overwhelming anxiety that interferes with their daily lives and prevents them from performing normal activities or maintaining healthy interpersonal relationships.

There are several types of anxiety disorders, including Generalized Anxiety Disorder (GAD), Panic Disorder, Phobias, Social Anxiety Disorder, and Agoraphobia. In generalized anxiety disorder, sufferers experience persistent worries and fears about various areas of life, even when there are no obvious threats. Panic disorder is characterized by recurrent panic attacks that occur suddenly and are accompanied by intense physical and psychological symptoms. Phobias are excessive and irrational fears of certain objects, situations, or activities, while social anxiety disorder involves excessive fear of social situations and negative evaluations by others. Agoraphobia refers to the fear of certain places or situations where it might be difficult or embarrassing to flee or get help when unexpected or unpleasant symptoms appear.

The causes of anxiety disorders are complex and can include biological, genetic, psychological, and environmental factors. A family predisposition can increase the risk of anxiety disorders, as can certain neurobiological factors such as chemical imbalances in the brain or disorders in the functioning of the limbic system, which is responsible for regulating emotions.

Psychological factors such as traumatic experiences, chronic stress, personality traits or unfavorable parenting patterns can also contribute to the development of anxiety disorders.

Treatment for anxiety disorders involves a combination of psychotherapy, medication, and self-help strategies. Cognitive behavioral therapy (CBT) has proven to be particularly effective, as it helps sufferers identify and change their irrational thought patterns, as well as learn coping strategies to deal with anxiety triggers. Medications such as selective serotonin reuptake inhibitors (SSRIs), benzodiazepines, or beta-blockers may be prescribed to relieve symptoms and improve emotional regulation. Self-help strategies such as regular physical activity, stress management techniques, relaxation exercises, and social support can also be helpful in dealing with anxiety symptoms.

AUTISM

ICD-10 Code: F84.0

Autism, also known as autism spectrum disorder (ASD), is a neurodevelopmental disorder that typically manifests in early childhood and is characterized by impaired social interaction, repetitive behavioral patterns, and limited communication skills. Autism is a broad spectrum of disorders, which means that the symptoms and their severity can vary greatly from person to person.

The core symptoms of autism include difficulty in social interaction, such as difficulty building relationships, difficulty understanding other people's emotions, and difficulty responding to social cues or nonverbal communication. Repetitive behavior and limited interests are also common features of autism, which can manifest itself in stereotypical behaviors, obsessive interest in certain topics or activities, and rigid routines.

Limitations in verbal and nonverbal communication are also typical of autism, with some individuals having difficulty developing or understanding language, while others may have difficulty with nonverbal communication such as eye contact or gesticulation.

The causes of autism are complex and can include a combination of genetic, environmental, and developmental causes. Genetic factors are thought to play a role, as autism can run in families, but environmental factors such as birth complications, exposure to certain chemicals, or infections during pregnancy may also play a role. There is no clear evidence that vaccinations cause autism.

The diagnosis of autism is made through a thorough assessment by professionals in the field of child development, such as pediatricians, psychiatrists, psychologists or specialized therapists. This may include behavioral observations, standardized testing, developmental and family history, and a physical exam.

Treatment for autism focuses on addressing the individual needs of the affected child or adult and providing support for the development of social skills, communication, and behavior management. Early interventions, such as early childhood education, behavioral therapy, speech therapy, and occupational therapy interventions, can help alleviate symptoms. Support from multidisciplinary care teams, including doctors, therapists, teachers, and family members, is critical to addressing the individual needs of people with autism.

BABY BLUES
ICD-10 Code: F53

The term "baby blues" refers to a temporary period of emotional lability and mood swings that many women experience after giving birth to a child. This phase usually occurs in the first days or weeks after delivery and can manifest itself through feelings of sadness, irritability, anxiety, fatigue and overwhelm.

The causes of the baby blues are many and can include hormonal changes, lack of sleep, stress, physical recovery after childbirth, adapting to the new role as a mother, and other factors. The transition to motherhood is a significant life change that can be associated with a variety of emotions, and it is normal for women to go through a certain period of emotional adjustment during this period.

Although the baby blues are temporary for most women and subside on their own, they can still be distressing and affect well-being. It's important that women experiencing the baby blues allow themselves and their feelings to give time and accept support. Family, friends, and professional caregivers can play an important role by providing emotional support, practical help, and encouragement.

The baby blues are to be distinguished from postpartum depression, a more serious form of mood disorder that can last longer and have more severe symptoms. Postpartum depression requires professional treatment and can have a negative impact on the bond between mother and child, as well as the well-being of the entire family.

If the symptoms of the baby blues persist or increase for more than a few weeks, or if a woman feels that she is unable to care for herself or her baby, it is important to seek medical help. Early intervention can help prevent or treat postpartum depression and promote the well-being of both mother and baby.

BINGE EATING DISORDER

ICD-10 Code: F50.8

Binge eating disorder (BED) is an eating disorder characterized by recurrent episodes of overeating, in which a person consumes large amounts of food in a short period of time while experiencing the feeling of loss of control. These binge eating attacks are often accompanied by strong feelings of shame, guilt, and discomfort.

People with binge eating disorder often use food as a coping mechanism to deal with emotional distress, stress, boredom, loneliness, or other difficult feelings. Unlike bulimia, binge eating disorder does not involve regular attempts to compensate for eating by vomiting, exercising excessively, or engaging in other behaviors.

The symptoms of binge eating disorder can lead to significant health problems, including overweight, obesity, diabetes, cardiovascular disease, high blood pressure, and psychological distress such as depression and anxiety. People with BED can also suffer from severe self-esteem problems, social isolation, and impaired quality of life.

The causes of binge eating disorder are varied and can include genetic, biological, psychological, and environmental factors. Some people may have a genetic predisposition to eating disorders, while others may be at risk from early life events, traumatic experiences, family dynamics, or cultural influences.

Treatment for binge eating disorder usually involves a combination of psychotherapy, nutritional counseling and, if necessary, medical treatment. Cognitive behavioral therapy (CBT) is a commonly used form of psychotherapy that aims to identify and change the underlying patterns of thought and behavior that contribute to binge eating. Medications such as antidepressants can also be used to treat concomitant mental illnesses.

BIPOLAR DISORDER

ICD-10 Code: F31

Bipolar disorder, formerly known as manic depression, is a serious mental illness characterized by extreme mood swings that alternate between manic and depressive episodes. People with bipolar disorder experience intense emotional states that can significantly affect their daily lives.

In manic episodes, sufferers experience an intense feeling of euphoria, excessive self-confidence, energy, and activity. They may exhibit impulsive behaviors, such as overspending, high-risk ventures, excessive use of alcohol or drugs, impulsive sexual behavior, and lack of impulse control. Manic episodes can also be accompanied by decreased sleep quality, restlessness, racing thoughts, and increased urge to talk.

Depressive episodes in bipolar disorder are similar to those in major depressive disorder and can be accompanied by strong feelings of sadness, hopelessness, worthlessness, lack of energy, sleep disturbances, changes in appetite, concentration problems and suicidal thoughts. Depressive episodes can cause a person to withdraw, isolate themselves from others, and have difficulty coping with everyday tasks.

The causes of bipolar disorder are not yet fully understood, but it is believed that genetic, biological, neurochemical, and environmental factors may play a role. People with a family history of bipolar disorder or other mood disorders are at increased risk of developing the disease.

Treatment for bipolar disorder involves a combination of medication and psychotherapy. Mood-stabilizing medications such as lithium, anticonvulsants, and atypical antipsychotics are often used to treat and prevent manic and depressive episodes. Psychotherapeutic approaches such as cognitive behavioral therapy (CBT), interpersonal therapy (IPT), and family therapy can help develop coping strategies, improve mood stability, and reduce the risk of relapse.

Coping with bipolar disorder often requires lifelong treatment and self-management strategies. Regular medical check-ups, self-monitoring, adherence to treatment plans, and support from family members, friends, and support groups are critical to long-term management of the condition.

BORDERLINE PERSONALITY DISORDER / EMOTIONALLY UNSTABLE PERSONALITY DISORDER
ICD-10 Code: F60.3

Borderline personality disorder is a mental illness characterized by unstable moods, interpersonal relationships, and self-image. People with borderline personality disorder may experience strong emotional outbursts, impulsivity, instability in relationships with other people, identity insecurity, and a sense of emptiness.

The symptoms of borderline personality disorder can show up in various areas of life, including:

- Emotional instability: Individuals with BPD often experience intense and rapid mood swings, which can range from extreme joy to deep despair. These mood swings can occur spontaneously or be triggered by events in their environment.
- Unstable interpersonal relationships: People with BPD often struggle to maintain stable and satisfying relationships. They may have idealizing or derogatory views of other people and quickly move back and forth between extreme attitudes.

- Identity insecurity: Individuals with borderline personality disorder may have an unstable self-image and have difficulty defining their goals, values, and interests. They may frequently wonder who they really are or what they want in life.

- Impulsivity: Impulsive behavior, such as excessive alcohol or drug use, risky sexual behavior, rash spending of money, or binge eating, is common in people with BPD.

- Feeling of emptiness: Many people with borderline personality disorder experience a chronic feeling of emptiness and inner emptiness that can be difficult to bear and often leads to self-harm or suicidal thoughts.

The causes of borderline personality disorder are multifactorial and include genetic, biological, neurochemical, psychological, and environmental factors. Early trauma, abuse, or neglect in childhood can increase the risk of developing BPD.

Treatment for borderline personality disorder involves a combination of psychotherapy, medication, and supportive interventions. Dialectical behavioral therapy (DBT) is a commonly used form of psychotherapy that aims to improve emotional regulation, interpersonal skills, and coping with impulses. Medications can be used to treat accompanying symptoms such as depression, anxiety, or mood swings.

Treatment for borderline personality disorder can be lengthy and difficult, but it requires intensive support from professionals, as well as the support of family and friends.

BRAIN-ORGANIC PSYCHOSYNDROME
ICD-10 Code: F07.9

Brain-organic psychosyndrome, also known as organic psychosyndromes or organic brain pathologies, refers to a group of mental and behavioral disorders caused by organic brain lesions or disorders. These disorders occur due to damage or dysfunction of the brain due to traumatic brain injury, neurodegenerative diseases, strokes, brain tumors, infections, toxic exposures, or other neurological diseases.

Characteristic of the brain-organic psychosyndrome are cognitive, emotional and behavioral disorders that can be traced back to the organic brain injury or disorder. Symptoms may include memory problems, difficulty concentrating, impaired attention, confusion, disorientation, speech and thinking disorders, personality changes, emotional lability, impulsivity, and decreased judgment.

Symptoms and severity can vary depending on the type, location, and extent of brain damage. Some people may have only mild cognitive impairment, while others may experience severe impairments in mental functions that significantly affect their ability to self-care and function on a daily basis.

The diagnosis of cerebral psychosyndrome requires a comprehensive neurological and psychiatric evaluation, including medical history, physical examination, neuropsychological tests, brain imaging, and laboratory tests. Diagnosis can often be challenging, as symptoms can be variable and non-specific, and can mimic other mental disorders or medical conditions.

Treatment for brain-organic psychosyndromes focuses on alleviating symptoms, improving quality of life, and maximizing the patient's ability to function. This may include a combination of medical treatment, psychotherapy, rehabilitation, support from caregivers and family members, lifestyle adjustments, and support services.

Coping with brain-organic psychosyndrome often requires long-term support and care, as symptoms are often chronic and can change over time.

BULIMIA

ICD-10 Code: F50.2

Bulimia is an eating disorder characterized by recurrent episodes of binge eating and subsequent behavior to compensate. People with bulimia feel that they are losing control over their eating habits and consuming large amounts of food in a short period of time. This is often referred to as binge eating. An eating binge is often followed by compensatory behavior, such as self-induced vomiting, excessive physical activity, abuse of laxatives or diuretics, or fasting.

The binge eating can be accompanied by a feeling of loss of control, as well as feelings of guilt, shame and fear of gaining weight. People with bulimia may try to keep their eating habits and weight problems a secret, which can lead to isolated behavior. Unlike anorexia nervosa, people with bulimia often have their weight within the normal range or even above average, but they may still have an intense fear of gaining weight.

The causes of bulimia are complex and include genetic, biological, psychological, and social factors. Some people may have a genetic predisposition to eating disorders, while others may be at risk from factors such as perfectionism, low self-esteem, family dynamics, traumatic experiences, or societal pressures and beauty ideals.

Bulimia is treated through a combination of psychotherapy, medical monitoring and nutritional counseling. Cognitive behavioral therapy (CBT) is a regularly used form of psychotherapy that aims to identify and change the patterns of thought and behavior that contribute to bulimia. In some cases, medication can be used to treat comorbidities such as depression or anxiety disorders.

BURNOUT SYNDROME

ICD-10 Code: Z73.0

Burnout syndrome is a state of chronic exhaustion and emotional exhaustion that arises from excessive stress in the workplace. It affects people in various professions and can have both physical and psychological effects. Burnout syndrome is often caused by a combination of workload, overwhelm, lack of recognition, and a sense of dissatisfaction with work.

Symptoms of burnout syndrome can include a variety of physical, emotional, and behavioral signs. These include chronic fatigue, exhaustion, sleep disorders, irritability, cynicism, disillusionment, feelings of hopelessness, concentration problems, increased mistakes at work, social withdrawal, and a loss of interest in work.

The causes of burnout are diverse and can include individual, professional and organizational factors.

Individual risk factors include high workloads, insufficient resources, lack of support in the workplace, lack of autonomy, unfavorable working conditions, interpersonal conflicts, unclear role expectations, and lack of reward or recognition.

Treatment for burnout involves a combination of self-care, stress management, psychotherapy, and possibly medical treatment. It is important for those affected to learn stress management techniques and integrate them into everyday life, such as regular exercise, sufficient sleep, healthy eating, relaxation exercises and setting boundaries.

Psychotherapy, especially cognitive behavioral therapy (CBT) or mindfulness-based therapies, can help identify and change negative thought patterns, develop coping strategies, and improve self-awareness. In some cases, medications may be prescribed to treat symptoms such as depression or anxiety in the short term.

The prevention of burnout often involves measures at the individual, organizational and societal level. Employers can foster a supportive work environment that offers autonomy, flexibility, social support, and opportunities for professional development. Individuals can review their workload, priorities, and work patterns, set boundaries, and respect themselves.

COMPULSIVE DISORDER

ICD-10 Code: F42

Obsessive-compulsive disorder is a serious mental illness characterized by the presence of obsessive thoughts and/or compulsive actions that significantly interfere with daily life. Obsessive thoughts are recurrent, unwanted, and often distressing thoughts or ideas that persist and can cause the affected person to feel great anxiety or anxiety. Compulsive actions are repetitive behaviors or rituals that are performed repeatedly, often in response to obsessive thoughts, to alleviate anxiety or prevent a feared disaster.

The topics of obsessive thoughts and actions can be diverse and range from cleanliness and hygiene constraints to constraints regarding symmetry and order to aggressive or obscene thoughts. The affected person often realizes that their compulsive thoughts and actions are irrational, but they still feel compelled to give in to them to relieve the anxiety or anxiety they cause.

Obsessive-compulsive disorder can have a significant impact on daily life, including interpersonal relationships, job performance, and overall quality of life. Sufferers may have difficulty coping with their daily lives, meeting their work or school obligations, and performing normal social activities without being affected by their obsessive thoughts and actions.

The causes of OCD are not fully understood, but it is believed that a combination of genetic, neurobiological, psychological, and environmental factors may play a role. Early life experiences, traumatic events, and neurochemical imbalances in the brain can all contribute to the development of OCD.

Treatment for obsessive-compulsive disorder usually involves a combination of drug therapy and psychotherapy. Selective serotonin reuptake inhibitors (SSRIs) and tricyclic antidepressants are often used to treat obsessive-compulsive disorder, while cognitive behavioral therapy (CBT), exposure and response prevention (ERP), and other forms of psychotherapy can help change negative thought patterns and develop coping strategies.

Treatment for OCD often requires patience and dedication because symptoms can persist in the long term, but with proper support, successful management is possible.

DELIRIUM

ICD-10 Code: F05

Delirium, also known as acute confusion syndrome, is a state of sudden and temporary confusion, disorientation, and impairment of attention and thinking. People with delirium may experience disorientation to the time, place, and person, have difficulty thinking clearly, and may exhibit confusion about their surroundings or situation.

Delirium is common in older adults, especially those who are hospitalized or have an acute medical condition. It can also occur in people with a history of dementia, brain injury, neurological disorders, alcohol or drug withdrawal, or other underlying health conditions.

Symptoms of delirium can vary from mild to severe and can develop quickly or progress slowly. These include disorientation, confusion, restlessness, hallucinations, delusions, uncoordinated movements, disturbed sleep-wake cycle, changes in behavior or personality, and a general impairment of cognitive function.

The causes of delirium are varied and can be triggered by a number of factors, including medical conditions such as infections, metabolic disorders, dehydration, drug or drug interactions, withdrawal from alcohol or drugs, brain injury, stroke, or surgery.

Treatment for delirium focuses on identifying and treating the underlying causes, as well as relieving symptoms and supporting the patient during delirium. This may include adjusting medications, treating infections or other medical problems, avoiding sleep deprivation or dehydration, promoting a calming environment, and assisting with orientation and communication.

The prognosis of delirium depends on the underlying cause, the severity of symptoms, and timely treatment. In many patients, delirium is transient and symptoms disappear when the underlying cause is resolved. For others, delirium may last longer and require more extensive treatment and support to promote recovery and minimize potential complications.

DELUSION

ICD-10 Code: F22

Delusion is a psychological symptom characterized by firm and unshakable beliefs that do not correspond to reality, even if they are obviously irrational or absurd. People who suffer from delusions hold on to their beliefs despite evidence to the contrary and are often unable to change their thoughts, even if they are irrational or unrealistic.

Delusions can include various topics, including:

1. Megalomania: A person may believe that they have extraordinary abilities, power, wealth, or knowledge that are superhuman.
2. Paranoia: A person may believe that they are being followed, monitored, eavesdropped, or threatened, even if there is no objective evidence of such persecution.
3. Jealousy delusion: A person may be convinced that their partner is cheating on them even though there is no evidence or evidence of it.
4. Reference compulsion: A person may believe that everyday events or random occurrences have a special meaning for them, even if they don't.

The causes of delusions can be varied and can be related to mental illnesses such as schizophrenia, bipolar disorder, organic brain disorders, substance abuse, or certain personality disorders. Neurobiological factors, genetic predispositions, environmental factors, traumatic experiences or stress can also play a role.

Delusion treatment aims to treat the underlying mental disorder and relieve symptoms. This may include a combination of drug therapy, such as antipsychotics or mood stabilizers, and psychotherapy, such as cognitive behavioral therapy (CBT) or psychoeducational interventions. In some cases, inpatient treatment may be necessary to stabilize acute symptoms and provide a safe environment.

People with delusions often have little insight into their condition and may not accept or seek treatment. In such cases, support from close people, relatives or professional caregivers can be important to ensure the best possible care and support.

DEMENTIA

ICD-10 Code: F03

Dementia is an umbrella term for a group of conditions that affect a person's cognitive function and daily functioning. It is not a specific disease, but a syndrome that includes a variety of symptoms, including memory loss, impaired thinking, loss of language skills, problems with planning and performing tasks, disorientation, changes in personality, and problems with judgment.

The most common form of dementia is Alzheimer's disease, but there are other types of dementia as well, including vascular dementia, Lewy body dementia, frontotemporal dementia, and mixed dementia. Each type of dementia has its own characteristic features and causes, but they all lead to a progressive loss of cognitive function and significantly affect the daily life of those affected.

The exact causes of dementia are not fully understood, but they are often the result of a combination of genetic, biological, and environmental factors. In some forms of dementia, such as Alzheimer's disease, abnormal protein deposits in the brain play a role, which can lead to damage to nerve cells and loss of brain functions.

The symptoms of dementia develop slowly over a longer period of time and worsen over time. In the early stages, symptoms can be subtle and limited to memory problems or slight changes in thinking and behavior, while in later stages they become more frequent and severe, leading to a loss of ability to perform even basic activities of daily living.

Diagnosing dementia requires a comprehensive assessment of cognitive function, including physical exams, brain imaging, blood tests, and neuropsychological tests. An accurate diagnosis can help identify the underlying cause of dementia and provide appropriate treatment and support.

Treatment for dementia focuses on relieving symptoms, slowing the progression of the disease, and improving the quality of life of those affected. These include medication to relieve symptoms, cognitive therapies, supportive therapies such as physical therapy or occupational therapy, lifestyle adjustments, and support for caregivers and family members.

Coping with dementia requires a comprehensive approach that includes medical treatment, psychosocial support, and practical help.

DEPRESSION

ICD-10 Code: F32

Depression is a common mental illness characterized by persistent feelings of sadness, hopelessness, depression, and a loss of interest in activities that used to bring joy. It is more than just occasional sadness and can significantly affect daily life.

Symptoms of depression can vary, but they can include physical, emotional, and cognitive signs. These include depressed mood, decreased drive, exhaustion, difficulty sleeping, changes in appetite, problems concentrating, feelings of worthlessness or guilt, suicidal thoughts or attempts, and physical ailments such as headaches or stomach problems.

The causes of depression are extensive and can include genetic, biological, psychological, and environmental factors. An imbalance of neurotransmitters in the brain, such as serotonin, dopamine and norepinephrine, often plays a role. Life events such as loss, trauma, relationship difficulties, financial problems, or chronic stress can also increase the risk of depression.

Treatment for depression usually involves a combination of psychotherapy, medication, and supportive interventions. Cognitive behavioral therapy (CBT) is a commonly used form of psychotherapy that aims to identify and change negative thought patterns, develop new coping strategies, and improve problem-solving skills. Antidepressants can be used to treat depression by balancing the neurotransmitters in the brain.

Coping with depression often requires time, patience, and support from professionals, family, and friends. Self-care strategies such as regular exercise, a healthy diet, getting enough sleep, social activities, time outdoors, and stress management can also be helpful.

With proper treatment and support, most people with depression can relieve their symptoms and live a fulfilling life.

DISORDERS IN SEXUAL BEHAVIOR

ICD-10 Code: F65

Sexual behavior disorders are a wide range of mental illnesses that affect a person's sexual function, desire, or behavior, and can lead to personal suffering, relationship problems, or legal consequences. These disorders can take different forms and have different causes.

Sexual behavior disorders include:

1. Sexual dysfunction: These disorders affect a person's ability to feel sexual pleasure or enjoy sexual activity. These include erectile

dysfunction, premature ejaculation, female sexual arousal disorder, and orgasm disorders.

2. Paraphilias: Paraphilias are abnormal or unusual sexual interests or preferences that lead to repeated and intense sexual fantasies, needs, or behaviors. These include fetishism, exhibitionism, voyeurism, pedophilia, sadistic or masochistic disorders, and transvestism.

3. Hypersexuality: Hypersexuality, also known as sex addiction or compulsive sexual behavior, is characterized by an excessive desire for sexual activity that leads to impaired quality of life, interpersonal relationships, or job functions.

4. Sexual pain disorders: These disorders are characterized by pain during sexual intercourse or sexual activity and can have physical, emotional, or psychological causes.

The causes of sexual behavior disorders can be diverse and can include biological, psychological, social, or environmental factors. These include genetic predispositions, hormonal imbalances, neurological diseases, early traumatization, interpersonal conflicts, relationship problems, cultural influences or unhealthy coping mechanisms.

Treatment of sexual behavior disorders usually involves a combination of drug therapy, psychotherapy, and behavioral interventions. Medication can be helpful in the treatment of sexual dysfunction or concomitant mental disorders. Psychotherapy, such as cognitive behavioral therapy (CBT), sexual therapy, or couples therapy, can help understand, process, and manage problematic sexual behaviors. Behavioral interventions may aim to reduce or control harmful sexual behaviors and build healthy sexual relationships.

Early diagnosis and treatment of sexual behavior disorders is important to alleviate personal suffering, improve relationship problems, and avoid legal consequences. It is important to seek professional help and talk openly about sexual problems in order to receive the best possible treatment and support.

DISORDERS IN SOCIAL BEHAVIOR

ICD-10 Code: F91-F94

Social behavior disorders are mental illnesses characterized by repetitive and persistent behavior that is socially inappropriate, disruptive, or aggressive, and that violates the rights of others or disregards their social norms or rules. These disorders typically occur during childhood or adolescence and can include a variety of behaviors.

The most common disorders in social behavior include:

1. Oppositional Defiant Disorder (ODD): In ODD, a person exhibits a persistent pattern of defiance,

rebelliousness, rebelliousness, quarrelsomeness, and disobedience to authority figures. These children or adolescents can often be argumentative, break the rules, blame others, or be irritable or angry.

2. Attention deficit hyperactivity disorder (ADHD): Although ADHD is primarily an attention disorder, affected children or adolescents may also have problems with impulsive behavior, hyperactivity, and social disruptive behavior, which can lead to conflict with others.

3. Disruptive Mood Dysregulation Disorder (DMDD): DMDD is characterized by pronounced emotional outbursts, irritable mood, and inappropriate behavior, which often lead to serious interpersonal problems or conflicts.

4. Difficulty concentrating: Children or adolescents with difficulty concentrating may have difficulty following rules, understanding social norms, or

responding appropriately to social cues or stimuli.

The causes of social behavior disorders can be diverse and can include genetic, biological, psychological, social, or environmental factors. These include genetic predispositions, early childhood trauma, unhealthy family structures, abuse or neglect, lack of social support, unfavorable living conditions, or inadequate parenting practices.

The treatment of social behavior disorders aims to stabilize behavior, reduce problematic behaviors, and develop healthy social skills. This may include a combination of behavioral interventions, family therapy, individualized therapy, social skills training, parent counseling, or specialized school programs.

DISSOCIATIVE DISORDERS

ICD-10 Code: F44

Dissociative disorders are a group of mental disorders characterized by a disorder of the normal integration of thoughts, identity, consciousness, memory, or perception. People with dissociative disorders may feel that their thoughts, feelings, or sensory perceptions are separate or disconnected from their normal consciousness.

There are several types of dissociative disorders, including:

1. Dissociative Identity Disorder (DID): Formerly known as multiple personality disorder, DID is characterized by the presence of two or more separate personalities or identities within a person. Each identity can have different memories, behaviors, and identity characteristics.

2. Dissociative amnesia: This disorder involves sudden memory loss for important personal information or events that are not due to normal forgetfulness. Amnesia can occur episodically and affect memories of trauma or stressful events.

3. Depersonalization/derealization disorder: People with this disorder experience feelings of alienation or detachment from their own body (depersonalization) or environment (derealization). They may feel as if they are living in a dream or that reality seems unreal.

4. Other dissociative disorders: This includes other dissociative symptoms or phenomena that cannot be specifically assigned to one of the above categories.

The causes of dissociative disorders can be due to traumatic events, such as abuse, neglect, or other forms of trauma in childhood or adulthood. Dissociative symptoms can act as a coping mechanism to cope with unbearable stress or emotional overload.

Treatment for dissociative disorders usually consists of a combination of psychotherapy, medication and supportive interventions. Psychotherapeutic approaches such as cognitive behavioral therapy (CBT), dialectical behavioral therapy (DBT), and eye movement desensitization and reprocessing (EMDR) can help manage the dissociative symptoms associated with traumatic experiences and promote the integration of thoughts and feelings.

Coping with dissociative disorders often requires time, patience, and support from professionals, family, and friends. Those affected should learn to develop healthy coping strategies, regulate their emotions and strengthen their sense of security.

DRUG ADDICTION

ICD-10 Code: F11.1

Drug addiction, also known as drug dependence or drug abuse, is a mental disorder characterized by compulsive, uncontrolled, and repeated cravings for certain medications. These medications can include both prescription and over-the-counter drugs. People who suffer from drug addiction use medication despite the negative impact on their physical health, interpersonal relationships, and quality of life.

A person affected by drug addiction may exhibit a variety of behaviors that indicate that they are addicted. These include, for example, searching for repeated prescriptions, visiting several doctors to prescribe medications, concealing consumption from others, neglecting personal responsibilities in favor of medication use, and experiencing withdrawal symptoms when consumption is stopped.

The causes of drug addiction can include genetic, biological, psychological, and social factors. People may turn to drug addiction for a variety of reasons, such as seeking relief from physical pain, coping with stress or emotional problems, craving euphoric feelings, or simply out of curiosity.

Treatment for drug addiction usually requires a comprehensive approach that combines medical, psychological, and social interventions. These include detoxification programs, drug therapies, psychotherapy, support groups, and the development of healthy coping strategies. The process of recovering from drug addiction can be lengthy and often requires long-term commitment.

EATING DISORDERS

ICD-10 Code: F50

Eating disorders are mental illnesses that manifest themselves through disturbed eating habits and an unhealthy relationship with food, body weight or body shape. They can be life-threatening and have a significant impact on the physical health, mental well-being and quality of life of those affected.

There are several types of eating disorders, including:

1. Anorexia nervosa: People with anorexia nervosa have an intense fear of gaining weight and a disturbed perception of their body weight and shape. You can take drastic measures to lose weight, such as excessive fasting, excessive physical activity, or abuse of laxatives or diuretics.

2. Bulimia nervosa: This eating disorder is characterized by recurrent episodes of binge

eating followed by compensatory behaviors, such as self-induced vomiting, excessive exercise, or abuse of laxatives or diuretics. People with bulimia often have a feeling of losing control over their eating behavior.

3. Binge eating disorder (BES): BES is similar to bulimia, but without the compensatory behavior. Individuals with BES experience recurrent episodes of binge eating, in which they consume large amounts of food in a short period of time, accompanied by a sense of loss of control and strong feelings of guilt or shame.

4. Eating disorder behavior without a specific diagnosis: This category includes various forms of disordered eating behavior that do not meet all the criteria for a particular eating disorder, such as restrictive diet, orthorectic behavior, or compulsive exercise.

The causes of eating disorders can include genetic, biological, psychological, social, and cultural factors. A combination of risk factors, such as genetic predisposition, low self-esteem, perfectionism, traumatic events, societal pressures, and ideal beauty standards, can increase the risk of developing an eating disorder.

The treatment of eating disorders requires a comprehensive approach that includes medical, psychotherapeutic and nutritional interventions. The goals of treatment include stabilizing weight, normalizing eating behaviors, managing underlying mental health issues, and improving self-esteem and quality of life.

Coping with eating disorders often requires time, patience, and support from professionals, family, and friends. Seeking professional help early is crucial, as eating disorders can be life-threatening, and timely treatment can improve the chances of recovery. Support groups and peer support can also be helpful in dealing with the challenges associated with eating disorders and promoting recovery.

HALLUCINATIONS

ICD-10 Code: R44.0

Hallucinations are sensory perceptions that occur in the absence of an external stimulus. They can occur in one or more of the five senses — sight, hearing, smell, taste, and touch — and may seem real to the affected person, although they are not caused by external stimuli. Hallucinations can occur with various mental illnesses, neurological disorders, substance abuse, or as a side effect of certain medications.

1. Visual hallucinations: These are hallucinations that affect vision and cause the affected person to see things that are not real. These can be

simple shapes, patterns, colors, or images ranging from people or objects to scenes.

2. Auditory hallucinations: These are hallucinations of hearing in which the affected person hears things that don't really exist. This can include hearing voices talking or commenting on the affected person, noises, music, or other sounds.

3. Olfactory hallucinations: These refer to hallucinations of the sense of smell, in which the affected person perceives odors that are not present. These can be pleasant or unpleasant odors that have no external origin.

4. Gustatory hallucinations: These are hallucinations of the sense of taste in which the affected person perceives tastes or aromas that are not real. This can cause the person to feel a certain taste in their mouth even though there is no food.

5. Tactile hallucinations: These refer to hallucinations of the sense of touch in which the

affected person perceives physical sensations, such as touch, tingling, crawling or pain that is not caused by external influences.

The causes of hallucinations can be varied and include mental illnesses such as schizophrenia, bipolar disorder, psychotic depression, substance abuse or withdrawal, sleep deprivation, neurological disorders, certain medications, or medical conditions such as dementia or epilepsy.

Treatment for hallucinations depends on the underlying cause and may include a combination of medical treatment, psychotherapy, medication, and supportive interventions. The goals of treatment are to relieve symptoms, improve quality of life, and manage the underlying condition.

HOSPITALISM

ICD-10 Code: F44.1

Hospitalism refers to the condition that occurs in children who have spent a long time in hospital, especially in institutions where they are separated from their primary caregivers. It is a historical term that originated in the early decades of the 20th century, when the effects of the separation of parents and caregivers on the development of children were studied.

The conditions that contribute to hospitalism include not only separation from primary caregivers, but also a lack of individual attention, stimulation, and emotional support, a highly routine environment, and limited social interaction. These factors can lead to a delay in emotional and physical development, as well as psychological problems such as depression, anxiety, and behavioral disorders.

Although the term "hospitalism" is less commonly used today, understanding the importance of attachment and emotional support in children's development has led hospitals and medical facilities to take steps to minimize the separation of children and their caregivers. This may include establishing parent participation programs, promoting family-centered care, and providing supportive services to families.

The term hospitalism clarifies the importance of a supportive and stimulating environment for children's development and emphasizes the need to minimize the separation of children and their caregivers in medical settings in order to promote their physical and emotional health. Today, the term is often used in the context of the history of child care and medical ethics to refer to past practices and emphasize the importance of child-centered approaches to health care.

HYSTERIA

ICD-10 Code: F44.6

Hysteria is a historical term that was originally used to describe a variety of unexplained or unusual symptoms that occurred primarily in women and were often thought of as a result of emotional or psychological distress. The term has taken on a variety of meanings over time and has been used in the past to describe a series of psychological and physical symptoms that are now viewed differently in different contexts.

Historically, hysteria has often been associated with the "weaker sex" and seen as an expression of female emotional instability or imbalance. The symptoms of hysteria could include a variety of physical ailments, such as paralysis, blurred vision, convulsions, difficulty breathing, or digestive problems, which were often without a clear medical cause.

With the advancement of medical science and the understanding of mental illness, the term hysteria has changed and is no longer used as a diagnostic category today. The symptoms that were once considered hysterical can now be considered part of other mental disorders, such as somatoform disorders, dissociative disorders or conversion disorders.

Historical concepts of hysteria were often associated with social and cultural notions of gender, power, and control, and were not necessarily based on scientific evidence. Nowadays, the term hysteria is avoided because it is stigmatizing, inaccurate, and does not meet current scientific standards.

Instead, modern approaches focus on studying and treating the underlying causes of physical and psychological symptoms, taking into account the biological, psychological, social, and cultural factors that can contribute to the emergence and maintenance of health problems.

INSOMNIA

ICD-10 Code: G47

Sleep disorders are impaired patterns in sleep that lead to lack of sleep or poor sleep quality. These disorders can take various forms, including difficulty falling asleep, staying asleep, or waking up early in the morning, as well as restless or non-restful nights.

Sleep disorders can have many causes, including stress, anxiety, depression, medical conditions, medication or drug abuse, unhealthy lifestyle habits or sleep environments, and sleep disorders such as sleep apnea or periodic limb movement disorder.

The impact of sleep disorders can be significant, affecting various aspects of daily life. These include fatigue and drowsiness during the day, impaired cognitive function, mood swings, irritability, concentration problems, impairment of work or school performance, and increased risk of accidents.

Treatment for sleep disorders depends on the underlying cause. This may include lifestyle changes, improved sleep hygiene, stress management, psychotherapy to treat concomitant mental illness, drug therapy, CPAP (Continuous Positive Airway Pressure) therapy for sleep apnea, or other treatments.

Early identification and treatment of sleep disorders is important to improve health and well-being and reduce the risk of serious secondary diseases.

INTERNET ADDICTION/ONLINE ADDICTION
ICD-10 Code: F63.9

Internet addiction, also known as internet addiction, online addiction, or problem internet use, is a form of behavioral addiction in which someone compulsively and excessively spends time on the internet, despite negative consequences for their mental health, interpersonal relationships, work obligations, or other areas of life.

Symptoms of internet addiction can be varied and include excessive internet use that interferes with time spent on other important activities, such as work, school, social interactions, or sleep. There is an inability to control the use of the Internet, despite the desire to spend less time on it. Withdrawal symptoms such as irritability, restlessness, anxiety or depression can occur if access to the Internet is restricted.

Despite negative consequences for mental health, interpersonal relationships, professional or school performance or financial situation, those affected continue to use the Internet. They often prefer the internet as a way to cope with stress, anxiety, or other emotional issues, neglecting personal commitments or social activities.

The causes of internet addiction can be complex and include a combination of biological, psychological, social, and environmental factors. Risk factors include genetic predisposition, mental health problems such as depression or social anxiety disorders, low self-esteem, high stress, boredom, social isolation, internet accessibility, and the attraction of online activities such as social media, gaming, or gambling.

Treatment for internet addiction includes a combination of psychotherapeutic approaches, behavioral therapy, cognitive behavioral therapy (CBT), support groups, family therapy, and, if necessary, medication to treat accompanying mental health problems such as depression or anxiety. Preventing internet addiction involves promoting healthy internet use, educating people about the risks and negative consequences of excessive internet use, promoting alternative activities and hobbies, promoting social support, and creating a balanced lifestyle.

KORSAKOFF SYNDROME

ICD-10 Code: F10.7

Korsakoff syndrome, also known as Korsakoff psychosis, is a serious neurological disorder characterized by memory problems, disorientation, confabulations (the creation of made-up stories to fill memory gaps), and difficulty learning and grasping new information. It often occurs as a complication of severe alcohol abuse and a deficiency of vitamin B1 (thiamine), known as Wernicke's encephalopathy.

Wernicke's encephalopathy is an acute neurological disease caused by a thiamine deficit in the brain that causes symptoms such as confusion, eye movement disorders, balance problems, and muscle weakness. If left untreated, it can progress and lead to Korsakoff syndrome.

The causes of Korsakoff syndrome are mostly associated with chronic alcohol abuse, as alcohol impairs thiamine metabolism and can lead to deficiency. In addition, a poor diet or an underlying gastrointestinal condition can also contribute to thiamine deficiency.

The symptoms of Korsakoff syndrome can vary, but they typically include:

1. Anterograde amnesia: Difficulty retaining and learning new information.
2. Retrograde amnesia: Memory loss for events and information before the disorder occurs.
3. Confabulations: The creation of invented stories to fill memory gaps.
4. Disorientation: Confusion about time, place, and situation.
5. Difficulty performing activities of daily living due to memory problems and disorientation.

The diagnosis of Korsakoff syndrome requires a comprehensive neurological evaluation, including medical history, physical examination, neuropsychological tests, and brain imaging. Treatment focuses on the administration of thiamine supplements to correct the deficiency, as well as the treatment of accompanying symptoms and rehabilitation to improve the quality of life of the sufferer.

The prognosis of Korsakoff syndrome depends on several factors, including the severity of the condition, response to treatment, and the patient's willingness to stop drinking alcohol.

MANIA

ICD-10 Code: F30

Mania is a central term in psychiatry that describes an extreme mood disorder characterized by persistent and overwhelming feelings of euphoria, excessive energy, and restlessness. People who suffer from mania often experience a significant change in their thinking, behavior, and perception that can severely affect their everyday lives.

A prominent feature of mania is an increased energy level, which manifests itself in an increased level of activity, an increased need to talk, and increased distractibility. Sufferers can relentlessly engage in various activities, act impulsively, and take excessive risks without considering the consequences.

The mood during mania is often extremely euphoric or irritable and can be accompanied by an exaggerated self-perception, which leads to excessive self-confidence and grandiose ideas. People in a manic state may feel invincible or invulnerable, believing that they have extraordinary abilities or powers.

However, the symptoms of mania can also be distressing, leading to problems in various areas of life, including interpersonal relationships, work performance, and financial stability. Sufferers may have difficulty concentrating, fulfilling responsibilities, and interacting appropriately with others, which can lead to significant stress and functional impairment.

Mania is a central feature of various mental illnesses, especially bipolar disorder, but it can also occur in the context of other disorders or be triggered by the abuse of substances. The causes of mania are complex and include genetic, neurochemical, and environmental factors.

Treatment for mania aims to stabilize symptoms and regulate mood to healthy levels. This may include a combination of drug therapy, especially mood stabilizers such as lithium or anticonvulsants, and psychotherapy to develop coping strategies and reduce the risk of relapse. Treatment is often carried out in close collaboration with a multidisciplinary treatment team to ensure comprehensive support.

NARCISSISM

ICD-10 Code: F60.81

Narcissism is a personality disorder characterized by an excessive need for admiration, a lack of empathy for others, and a strong sense of self-importance. People with narcissistic personality disorder often have an inflated ego and consider themselves exceptional or special. They tend to put themselves above others and expect special treatment and admiration, even if they have not performed well.

A central characteristic of narcissism is an excessive self-obsession, which manifests itself in a constant pursuit of attention, admiration, and praise. Narcissistic individuals can strongly identify with their physical appearance, social status, or achievements, and expect others to recognize and admire their grandiosity.

Despite their seemingly confident and superior appearance, people with narcissistic personality disorder can have profound insecurities and fragile self-esteem. They are often sensitive to criticism or rejection and can become aggressive or hurtful if they feel threatened in their self-perception.

Narcissistic personality disorder can affect various areas of life, including interpersonal relationships, work performance, and overall well-being. People with this disorder may have difficulty maintaining lasting and fulfilling relationships, as they tend to manipulate or take advantage of others to satisfy their own needs.

The causes of narcissistic personality disorder are not fully understood, but it is believed that both genetic and environmental factors may play a role. A combination of biological vulnerabilities, early life experiences, and individual personality traits may contribute to the development of this disorder.

Treatment for narcissistic personality disorder can be challenging, as people with this disorder often have little insight into their own problems and tend to reject therapeutic interventions. However, psychotherapy, especially cognitive behavioral therapy and psychodynamic therapy, can help alleviate symptoms and develop healthier coping strategies. However, the treatment process can be lengthy and often requires long-term therapeutic support.

NEUROSES

ICD-10 Code: F48

Neuroses are mental disorders characterized by persistent and distressing emotional symptoms that interfere with a person's daily life. Unlike psychosis, people with neurosis are usually able to recognize reality, but they can still suffer from severe emotional stress and unpleasant symptoms.

A common form of neurosis is generalized anxiety disorder, in which a person experiences chronic and excessive worry and anxiety that is not adequately related to the real threat situation. These fears can be widespread and extend to different areas of life, which can lead to a severe impairment of the quality of life.

Another form of neurosis is obsessive-compulsive disorder, in which people experience recurring obsessive thoughts or actions that they cannot control. These obsessive thoughts and actions can be extremely distressing, causing sufferers to constantly repeat certain rituals or behaviors to alleviate their anxiety.

Another common form of neurosis is somatoform disorder, in which physical symptoms occur for which no medical cause can be found. People with somatoform disorders may suffer from chronic pain, fatigue, or other physical ailments that interfere with their daily lives, even though there are no organic causes.

The causes of neuroses are diverse and can include genetic, biological, psychological, and environmental factors. Early life experiences, traumatic events, genetic predisposition, and personal vulnerabilities can all contribute to the development of neuroses.

The treatment of neuroses can include a combination of drug therapy and psychotherapy. Antidepressants, anxiety relievers, and other psychotropic medications can help relieve symptoms, while cognitive behavioral therapy, exposure and response prevention, and other forms of psychotherapy can help change negative thought patterns and develop coping strategies.

PANIC DISORDER

ICD-10 Code: F41.0

Panic disorder is a mental illness characterized by recurrent and unexpected panic attacks. These attacks are sudden moments of intense anxiety or restlessness, often accompanied by physical symptoms such as palpitations, sweating, tremors, shortness of breath and dizziness. People with panic disorder often live in constant fear of further panic attacks and can adjust their behavior accordingly to avoid potential triggers.

A panic attack can appear seemingly out of nowhere and can peak within a few minutes, causing sufferers to feel like they are losing control or dying. These intense physical symptoms can cause the affected person to feel extremely anxious or distressed and often seek medical help to ensure that there is no serious medical cause.

People with panic disorder can also suffer from constant fear of future panic attacks, which can lead to significant disruption in daily life. They may avoid certain places or situations that they associate with their previous panic attacks, and may even become socially isolated to avoid potentially distressing situations.

The causes of panic disorder are extensive and can include genetic, biological, psychological, and environmental factors. Some people develop panic disorder in response to stressful life events or traumatic experiences, while for others, genetic predisposition or biochemical dysregulation may play a role.

Treatment for panic disorder usually involves a combination of drug therapy and psychotherapy. Antidepressants, especially selective serotonin reuptake inhibitors (SSRIs) and benzodiazepines, can help relieve symptoms, while cognitive behavioral therapy (CBT) and exposure and response prevention (ERP) can help change negative thought patterns and develop coping strategies.

PARANOIA

ICD-10 Code: F22

Paranoia is a psychological condition characterized by excessive and irrational fear or distrust of others. People with paranoia often have a firm belief that other people want to harm them, observe or monitor them, without any evidence or actual threats.

Symptoms of paranoia can take a variety of forms, from mild distrust to pronounced delusions. Sufferers may believe that they are being followed by government agencies, intelligence agencies, neighbors, family members, or strangers. They may also feel that their thoughts are being controlled or manipulated, or that they are victims of a conspiracy.

Paranoia can lead to significant disruption in daily life, as the affected person may not be able to trust others, maintain relationships, or perform normal activities without feeling constantly threatened. This can lead to social isolation, withdrawal, and a strong sense of loneliness.

The causes of paranoia include genetic, biological, psychological, and environmental factors. Early life experiences, traumatic events, substance abuse, and mental illnesses such as schizophrenia can all contribute to the development of paranoia.

Treatment for paranoia often requires a multidisciplinary approach and may include a combination of drug therapy and psychotherapy. Antipsychotic medications can help relieve symptoms, especially if paranoia occurs as part of an underlying mental disorder such as schizophrenia. Psychotherapy, especially cognitive behavioral therapy (CBT) and support groups, can help change negative thought patterns, improve self-awareness, and develop healthy coping strategies.

PERSONALITY DISORDERS

ICD-10 Code: F60-F69

Personality disorders are a group of mental disorders characterized by persistent patterns of thinking, feeling, and behavior that deviate from the norm and can lead to suffering or impairment in various areas of life. These patterns are often deep-rooted and manifest in different situations over a longer period of time.

There are different types of personality disorders, each of which has its own characteristics and symptoms. Some of the most common personality disorders include:

1. Borderline personality disorder (BPD): characterized by unstable moods, impulsive behavior, intense interpersonal relationships, and a strong sense of emptiness.
2. Narcissistic personality disorder (NPS): characterized by inflated self-esteem, a constant

desire for admiration, lack of empathy for others, and a tendency to take advantage of others.

3. Avoidant personality disorder (VPS): characterized by excessive shyness, anxiety in social situations, avoidance of interpersonal relationships, and a strong sense of inadequacy.

4. Dependent personality disorder (APD): characterized by an extreme need for support and validation from others, lack of self-confidence, and a strong fear of rejection or abandonment.

5. Schizoid personality disorder (SPS): characterized by low emotional expression, social distancing, and limited interest in interpersonal relationships.

6. Histrionic personality disorder (HPS): characterized by exaggerated emotionality, dramatic behavior, a desire to be the center of attention, and a strong desire for attention and validation.

7. Obsessive-compulsive personality disorder (CPS): characterized by an excessive love of order, perfectionism, a need for control and rigid rules and routines.

The causes can include a combination of genetic, biological, psychological, social, and environmental factors. Early childhood experiences, traumatic events, family dynamics, and personality traits often play a role in their development.

Treatment for personality disorders often requires long-term psychotherapeutic intervention to examine and change the underlying patterns of thinking, feeling, and behavior. Approaches such as cognitive behavioral therapy (CBT), dialectical behavioral therapy (DBT), psychodynamic therapy, and group therapy can be helpful.

The prognosis of personality disorders varies depending on the type of disorder, the severity of symptoms, the individual's willingness to seek treatment and support, and other factors.

PHOBIA

ICD-10 Code: F40

Phobias are a type of anxiety disorder characterized by an excessive and unreasonable feeling of fear of certain objects, situations, or activities. These fears can be so intense that they can significantly affect the daily life of the affected person and lead to avoidance behaviors.

There are different types of phobias that can be divided into three main categories:

1. Specific phobias: These are phobias of certain objects, animals, situations, or activities. Some common examples include fear of heights (acrophobia), fear of spiders (arachnophobia),

fear of flying (aviophobia), fear of confined spaces (claustrophobia), or fear of injections (trypanophobia).

2. Social phobia: This phobia refers to an excessive fear of social situations or the fear of being watched or judged by others. People with social phobias may have difficulty talking, socializing, or being comfortable in groups in social situations.

3. Agoraphobia: This phobia refers to the fear of situations or places where it is difficult to flee or get help when you panic. People with agoraphobia often avoid crowded places, open spaces, or traveling alone.

Symptoms of phobias can vary, but they can include physical, emotional, and behavioral reactions. Physical symptoms may include tachycardia, sweating, trembling, shortness of breath, dizziness or nausea. Emotional symptoms can include extreme anxiety, panic, or a sense of unreality. Behavioral symptoms can include avoidance behavior, withdrawal or escape from the anxiety situation.

The causes are often the result of a combination of genetic, biological, psychological, and environmental factors. Traumatic experiences, negative childhood experiences, family history of phobias or anxiety disorders, and certain personality traits can increase the risk of developing a phobia.

Treatment of phobias can include a combination of psychotherapeutic approaches and, if necessary, medication. Psychotherapy, especially cognitive behavioral therapy (CBT) and exposure and response prevention therapy (ERP), can help identify, investigate, and overcome irrational fears. Medications such as anxiety relievers or antidepressants may also be prescribed to relieve symptoms.

POST-TRAUMATIC STRESS DISORDER (PTSD)

ICD-10 Code: F43.1

Post-traumatic stress disorder (PTSD) is a mental disorder that can occur after someone has experienced or witnessed a traumatic experience that poses a threat to their life or physical integrity. PTSD can occur in people of any age and can cause various symptoms that can significantly affect daily life.

The symptoms of PTSD can be divided into four main categories:

1. Reliving the trauma: People with PTSD may have recurring, distressing memories of the trauma, in the form of flashbacks, nightmares, or distressing thoughts and images. These memories can be so strong that they feel like the trauma is happening again.

2. Avoidance and numbness: People with PTSD may try to avoid thoughts, feelings, or

conversations that might remind them of the trauma. You could also try to avoid places, people, or activities that are associated with the trauma. Some people with PTSD may also have difficulty feeling positive emotions or showing interest in previous hobbies or activities.

3. Negative changes in thoughts and mood: This can manifest itself in memory problems, negative beliefs about oneself or others, feelings of guilt or shame, feelings of alienation from others, or a constant sense of threat.

4. Overarousal and increased irritability: People with PTSD may have difficulty concentrating, be easily irritable, have trouble sleeping, be overly alert, or get startled easily.

PTSD often arises as a result of a traumatic experience, such as physical or sexual abuse, natural disasters, serious accidents, war, terrorist attacks, or other life-threatening events. A variety of factors, including genetic, biological, psychological, and environmental factors, can increase the risk of developing PTSD.

Treatment for PTSD often involves a combination of psychotherapeutic approaches and, if necessary, medication. Psychotherapy, especially trauma therapy, cognitive behavioral therapy (CBT), and EMDR (Eye Movement Desensitization and Reprocessing), can help process traumatic memories and relieve symptoms. Medications such as antidepressants or anxiety relievers may also be prescribed to treat symptoms.

PSYCHOSES

ICD-10 Code: F20-F29

Psychosis is a serious psychological condition characterized by a loss of contact with reality. People who suffer from psychosis may experience symptoms such as hallucinations, delusions, disorganization of thought and speech, and disturbed behavior. These symptoms can significantly alter the affected person's perception of themselves, others and their environment and lead to impairments in daily life.

Hallucinations are sensory experiences that occur without any actual stimulus, such as hearing voices, seeing things that aren't there, or feeling touch that isn't there. Delusions are firm and unshakable beliefs that are maintained despite the lack of evidence or reality to the contrary. These can include paranoia, delusions of grandeur, religious or bizarre beliefs.

Psychosis can have a variety of causes, including genetic predisposition, neurochemical imbalances in the brain, neurological disorders, substance abuse, and traumatic life events. They can occur in the context of conditions such as schizophrenia, bipolar disorder, severe depression, drug-induced psychosis or other mental disorders.

Treatment of psychosis requires a comprehensive approach and may include a combination of drug therapy, psychotherapy, and supportive interventions. Antipsychotic medications are often used to treat hallucinations and delusions, while psychotherapy can help manage symptoms, improve functionality, and reduce the risk of relapse. The treatment approach can vary depending on individual needs and the underlying cause of psychosis, and close collaboration with a multidisciplinary treatment team is often required to ensure successful treatment.

SCHIZOAFFECTIVE DISORDER

ICD-10 Code: F25

Schizoaffective disorder is a mental illness that has characteristics of both schizophrenia and affective disorders such as depression or manic episodes. People with schizoaffective disorder may experience a combination of symptoms from both, including psychotic symptoms such as hallucinations or delusions, as well as mood disorders such as depression or mania.

The symptoms of schizoaffective disorder can be divided into three main categories: psychotic symptoms, affective symptoms, and disorders of thought or behavior.

Psychotic symptoms include hallucinations, delusions, disorganized thinking or speech, and unusual or bizarre behaviors.

Affective symptoms include mood changes that can be similar to those of depression or mania. This can include intense sadness, hopelessness, joylessness, or loss of interest and joy in depression, or increased energy, unusual activity, impulsive behavior, or excessive self-esteem in mania.

Disorders of thought or behavior can include unusual thoughts or beliefs, problems with concentration or attention, difficulty processing information, or unusual behaviors or movements.

The causes of schizoaffective disorder are not fully understood, but similar to schizophrenia and mood disorders, genetic, neurobiological, neurochemical, environmental, and psychosocial factors may play a role.

The treatment of schizoaffective disorders usually consists of a combination of drug therapy and psychotherapeutic approaches. Antipsychotics are often used to control psychotic symptoms, while mood stabilizers, antidepressants, or other medications can be used to treat mood symptoms. Psychotherapy, such as cognitive behavioral therapy (CBT), supportive therapy, or social skills training, can help manage symptoms and promote rehabilitation.

SCHIZOPHRENIA

ICD-10 Code: F20

Schizophrenia is a serious mental illness that affects a person's thinking, perception, emotions, and behavior. People with schizophrenia may experience different symptoms, which can be divided into three main categories: positive symptoms, negative symptoms, and cognitive symptoms.

Positive symptoms include perceptual disorders such as hallucinations (perceived sensory experiences without actual stimulus, typically auditory, visual, or olfactory) and delusions (fixed beliefs that do not correspond to reality). These symptoms can lead to disturbed thinking and behavior characterized by unusual or irrational beliefs, incoherent speech or behavior.

Negative symptoms include a decrease in emotional expression, social withdrawal, listlessness, impoverishment of speech and thinking, and lack of interest in social activities or relationships. These symptoms can lead to an impairment of daily functioning and quality of life.

Cognitive symptoms include impairments in attention, memory, processing speed, and problem-solving skills. These symptoms can make it difficult to complete tasks, process information, or focus on a task.

The causes of schizophrenia can include a combination of genetic, neurobiological, neurochemical, environmental, and psychosocial factors. Disruption of the dopamine system in the brain is often associated with schizophrenia, but other neurotransmitters such as glutamate may also play a role.

The treatment of schizophrenia usually consists of a combination of drug therapy and psychotherapeutic approaches. Antipsychotics are the main class of medications used to treat schizophrenia and aim to control positive symptoms and prevent relapse. Psychotherapy, such as cognitive behavioral therapy

(CBT), supportive therapy, or social skills training, can help manage symptoms, improve quality of life, and promote rehabilitation.

The prognosis for people with schizophrenia can vary, but early diagnosis, appropriate treatment, and ongoing support can help relieve symptoms and reduce the rate of relapse. A comprehensive approach that includes medical, psychotherapeutic and social support is often the most effective in managing this complex condition.

SELF-INJURIOUS BEHAVIOR
ICD-10 Code: F68.8

Self-injurious behavior (SVV) is a complex pattern of behavior in which a person intentionally causes damage to their own body without a desire to commit suicide.

These actions can take various forms, including cutting, burning, scratching, hitting, head-banging, or other methods of inflicting physical pain on oneself.

People who exhibit self-injurious behavior can use this as a coping mechanism to deal with severe emotional pain, inner emptiness, tension, anxiety, anger, or other psychological distress. SVV can be understood as an attempt to externalize or alleviate internal pain or emotional tension to a physical level by focusing on the physical pain.

SVV is often associated with other mental health problems, including depression, anxiety disorders, post-traumatic stress disorder (PTSD), eating disorders, borderline personality disorder, or other personality disorders.

The causes of self-injurious behavior can be varied and can include genetic, biological, psychological, social, and environmental factors. Traumatic experiences, abuse, neglect, emotional distress, interpersonal conflict, low self-esteem, inadequate coping skills, or other psychosocial stressors can increase the risk of SVV.

Treatment for self-injurious behavior aims to identify the underlying causes, develop alternative coping strategies, and improve emotion regulation skills. This can include a combination of psychotherapeutic approaches such as Dialectical Behavioral Therapy (DBT), Cognitive Behavioral Therapy (CBT), mindfulness exercises, trauma therapy, or other specialized treatments. In some cases, drug treatment can be used to treat concomitant mental disorders.

A supportive social environment, access to psychosocial resources, and involvement in support groups or peer support networks can also be important components of SVV treatment.

SOMATOFORM DISORDERS

ICD-10 Code: F45

Somatoform disorders are mental illnesses in which physical symptoms occur for which no adequate medical explanation can be found. People with somatoform disorders experience physical discomfort or symptoms that are significant and interfere with their lives but have no organic causes.

These disorders can take various forms, including:

1. Somatization disorder: In this disorder, a person experiences a variety of physical symptoms over a long period of time without a medical explanation being found. These symptoms can relate to different body systems, such as the gastrointestinal tract, the cardiovascular system, the nervous system, or the musculoskeletal system.

2. Conversion disorder: In this disorder, a person experiences sensory or motor symptoms that cannot be explained by a neurological disease. These symptoms may include paralysis, numbness, blindness, seizures, or movement disorders, and may come on suddenly or in episodes.

3. Pain disorder: In this disorder, a person experiences persistent and severe pain for which no adequate medical explanation can be found. This pain can occur in various places in the body and can lead to significant impairments in quality of life.

4. Hypochondriac disorder: In this disorder, a person has a persistent fear of a serious illness, although medical examinations show no signs of such a disease. The affected person often interprets normal physical sensations or minor symptoms as signs of a serious illness and

regularly seeks medical examinations or treatments.

A combination of genetic, biological, psychological, social and environmental factors can be assumed to be the cause. Previous traumatic experiences, stress, interpersonal conflicts, a lack of emotional support, or a low ability to cope with illness can increase the risk of somatoform disorders.

Treatment for somatoform disorders focuses on identifying the underlying psychological factors and managing the symptoms. This may include a combination of psychotherapy, including cognitive behavioral therapy (CBT), stress management techniques, relaxation exercises, mindfulness, or other specialized therapies, and medication if necessary.

A supportive social environment, access to psychosocial resources, and involvement in support groups can also be important components of treatment.

STALKING

ICD-10 Code: F60.3

Stalking is a pattern of behavior in which a person repeatedly and unintentionally pursues, monitors, or harasses another person, thereby triggering fear, stress, or feelings of threat in the affected person. Stalking can take various forms and can take place in person, via the internet or other electronic means of communication.

Typical behaviors of stalkers can be:

1. Physical tracking: The stalker can physically stalk the person by observing, stalking or ambushing them, whether at home, at work, at school or in public.

2. Making contact: The stalker can try to make contact with the affected person by calling, sending messages, writing emails, or communicating via social media. These contacts can be harassing, threatening, or overly intrusive.

3. Surveillance: The stalker can monitor the victim's activities, whereabouts, or life by tracking their movements, monitoring their social media, collecting private information, or using GPS trackers.

4. Threats or violence: In some cases, the stalker may commit threatening or violent acts against the affected person or their loved ones, which can lead to significant anxiety, stress, and danger.

Stalking can have a serious impact on the mental health, well-being and quality of life of the person affected. Possible consequences include anxiety, depression, sleep disorders, loss of confidence, social isolation, impaired work or school performance, suicidal thoughts or attempts, and physical injury.

The causes of stalking can include various psychological, social, or emotional factors, such as unhealthy relationship behaviors, unreasonable expectations, jealousy, need for control, revenge, mental disorders, or a disturbed idea of love.

Coping with stalking requires proper support and intervention. This may include contacting the police to report stalking, applying for a restraining order, securing a home or workplace, maintaining close relationships with support persons, or seeking psychotherapeutic support. It is important not to ignore or trivialize stalking, as it is a serious crime that can have serious consequences.

TRAUMA

ICD-10 Code: F43.9

Trauma is a psychological response to an event or experience that is perceived as overwhelming, threatening, or life-threatening, and that evokes intense emotional responses. Traumatic events can take various forms, including physical or sexual violence, accidents, natural disasters, war, abuse, neglect, the loss of a loved one, or serious illness.

Traumatic events can lead to a variety of psychological, emotional, and physical symptoms, including:

1. Post-traumatic stress disorder (PTSD): PTSD is a serious mental illness that can occur after someone has experienced a traumatic event. Symptoms may include flashbacks, nightmares, excessive anxiety, irritability, sleep disturbances, emotional numbness, avoidance behaviors, and increased jumpiness.

2. Complex post-traumatic stress disorder (CPTSD): CPTSD occurs when traumatic events occur over a prolonged period of time, such as long-term abuse, neglect, or repeated exposure to violence. In addition to those of PTSD, symptoms can also include disorders in self-image, difficulty

regulating emotions, problems with interpersonal relationships, and identity problems.

3. Depression and anxiety: Traumatic events can also lead to depression, anxiety disorders, or other mental health problems that can interfere with a person's daily functioning.

4. Physical symptoms: People who experience traumatic events may also develop physical ailments or medical conditions, such as sleep disorders, headaches, gastrointestinal problems, chronic pain, or cardiovascular disease.

The effects of trauma can be long-lasting and affect a person's life in a variety of ways. Not everyone who experiences a traumatic event develops PTSD or other mental health problems. The effects of trauma depend on various factors, including the nature of the event, duration, intensity, personal resilience, and coping mechanisms available.

Trauma treatment aims to alleviate symptoms, promote emotional processing of the event, and develop healthy coping strategies. This may include a combination of psychotherapy, medication, support groups, family therapy, relaxation techniques, and other supportive interventions.

Thank you for your interest in this book

The satisfaction of our readers is important to us, and we would be very happy if you could send us your feedback on the book.

We would like to ask you to take a moment to write a customer review on Amazon. In this way, you support other readers in making purchasing decisions and contribute to constantly improving our offer.

You are also welcome to use the following QR code:

IMPRESSUM
Information according to § 5 TMG:
Markus Gohlke
c/o IP-Management #16265
Ludwig-Erhard-Str. 18
20459 Hamburg
Contact:
E-mail: elcamondobeach@gmail.com
Phone: +491751555847
Imprint: Independently published

Made in the USA
Columbia, SC
07 December 2024

48699167R00072